4-2-3-1
Formation Specific Soccer Passing Patterns
&
Shadow Play Exercises
Stimulate Movement Ideas Using A Flexible Version of The 4-2-3-1 Formation

By Marcus DiBernardo

Introduction

Many coaches use passing patterns and shadow play exercises on a regular basis to increase technical ability, improve fitness levels, stimulate movement ideas, build discipline, increase focus, encourage coordinated timed multi-player movements and establish a group passing tempo. There is no doubt that passing patterns and shadow play exercises are valuable for player development. However, at some point it will become important to use specific patterns that directly fit the teams "Game Model". A "Game Model" is simply the way you want your team to play; it involves the team's style of play, identity and formation. The way you train at some point should specifically relate to the way you play (training model = game model). This book takes the 4-2-3-1 soccer formation and provides a series of passing patterns and shadow play exercises that directly relate to the teaching of a flexible 4-2-3-1 formation. When player's train using these patterns, they are simulating many of the movements and passing combinations they will encounter when playing the 4-2-3-1 formation in an actual game. I understand that no two coaches are the same and every coach will interpret formations in their own way unique way. However, I designed this book to teach the 4-2-3-1 formation in a fashion that I consider to be modern, flexible and fluid. The training exercises are intended to stimulate movement ideas for players by showing them the vast possibilities that are available by playing a flexible 4-2-3-1 system. Ultimately the goal is to encourage different players to fill different spaces though out the game, so players are not just filling the same old predictable spaces assigned to them. When a formation is played in a way that it is too robotic and ridged, with no real freedom of movement and interchanging of positions, it becomes predictable, less dynamic, boring and ultimately less effective. I prefer to let my players operate under the general umbrella of the 4-2-3-1 formation, while still allowing them the freedom to make their own movement decisions in order to exploit the opponent. The exercises presented in this book will aid you in teaching the concepts and ideas needed to be successful playing a fluid and flexible version of the 4-2-3-1 formation.

As always feel free to contact me at coachdibernardo@gmail.com with any questions or comments on the book. If you are interested in my online soccer instructor's cognitive development course please visit www.soccersmarttraining.com

Table of Contents

4-2-3-1 Center Midfield Players

In order to create and use meaningful passing patterns and shadow play exercises

that train the "4-2-3-1 System", it is imperative to have a very good understanding

of how the formation can be utilized. Lets start by looking at the heart of the

formation, the three center midfield players (#6,8,10). These three players can be

deployed in a variety different ways, lending to the flexibility and freedom of

movement offered in the formation. The idea is to allow different players the ability

to occupy different spaces, while still maintaining good team balance. If the same

players always operate in the same spaces, the opposition will have limited

problems to solve defensively, the game will become predictable, simple to read,

easy to defend and lack overall movement and sophistication. The first part of this

book covers different passing patterns intended to stimulate positioning and

movement ideas for the center midfielders within the framework of a 4-2-3-1

formation. However, keep in mind the organization and positioning of the midfield

and team will be in a state of constant change and continuous movement during the

flow of a game. Please do not take this book as a strict set of rigid plays and

movements to be trained like an "American Football" playbook, rather it is intended

to increase player awareness and raise the "Soccer IQ" of the players and coaches by

providing various options for player movements, rotations and over all team

organization & flexibility. I personally view the modern game of soccer as a free

flowing game that demands many interchanges of player positions that are carried

out within a flexible system called a formation. The modern player of the future will step on the field and be required be a thinker, the days of just being a worker in modern soccer will eventually come to an end. Teams in the modern game may play 2-6 players at the back, 2-6 players at midfield, 0-5 players up front and who knows how many will float between the lines, it will all depend on the situation (phase of the game). Whatever opportunities arise within the game, the players will have to be intelligent enough and have the freedom within the system to find ways to exploit those opportunities. One of the main keys to making modern soccer tactics work will be the development of intelligent and technically skilled players. The best example I can offer that exhibits flexibility of movement and player freedom within a framework would be the work done by Pep Guardiola at Bayern Munich. Listen to his players describe their style of play and you hear things like "its not the formation" or "sometimes we play with two 6's, one 6, two 10's, two 8's or even with just two players in the back" or "we don't really talk about the formations that much, its more about adapting & problem solving and carrying out concepts". My point is Pep Guardiola's players understand where the spaces are that need to be exploited and this can be done by any number of players within the framework he has created. Before getting into this books training methods, I want to reiterate one more time that the passing patterns and shadow play exercises presented in this book are meant to stimulate different movement patterns and organizational ideas within the broad framework of the 4-2-3-1 formation. This formation can easily be played in a more rigid traditional fashion but in my opinion that ultimately is less effective and not good for player development.

4-2-3-1 Passing Pattern Key Points

- Train the patterns in both directions. Patterns can be reversed every other repetition or after a series of repetitions.
- Make sure the movement between the passing and receiving player is coordinated and timed. The receiving player should be moving into the space as the ball arrives.
- Insist on correct foot passing and receiving.
- All passes must be firm.
- There should be eye contact between the passer and receiver.
- Be sure your body shape is correct in preparation to receive the incoming pass & execute a pass.

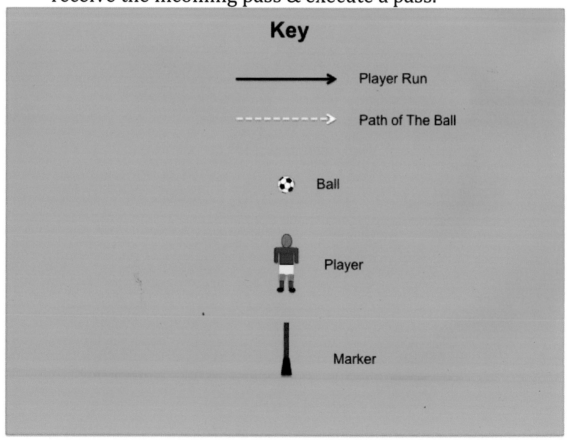

Center Midfield: 6-6-10 Variations

Lets start with the example of two center midfielders that are dropped deeper, both acting as #6's, while one center mid is kept high (#10). By dropping two players the advantage is that one player doesn't have to cover the entire width in front of the back four and it gives an additional option for rotating the ball side to side. Often the decision to have an additional center midfielder drop deeper depends on the type of pressure the opponents are exerting. If the defensive pressure is low there may be no need to drop a player back, if the pressure is high, more deep options may be needed.

To encourage flexible and fluid movement off the ball allow different players to occupy different spaces, interchange with each other and rotate positions with some freedom. This first pattern provides an example of how player rotation can work with the three center midfielders. The rotation is counterclockwise with the #6 becoming the #10, the #10 dropping into the #6's role and the other #6 rotating to the right. This rotation still leaves two #6's and a #10. Having the three midfielders rotate is more difficult for the opposing team to track defensively. The movement can confuse the defense, while opening up available spaces to play into. This pattern is meant to train rotation of the ball using two #6's and one #10 at midfield. The center backs will open-up, as the wingbacks will get high and wide. Every pattern should be trained in both directions. Players need to be comfortable receiving and passing with the left and the right foot.

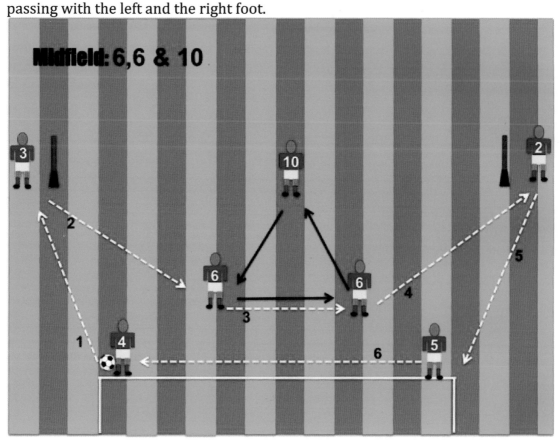

This is the same pattern done in the opposite direction.

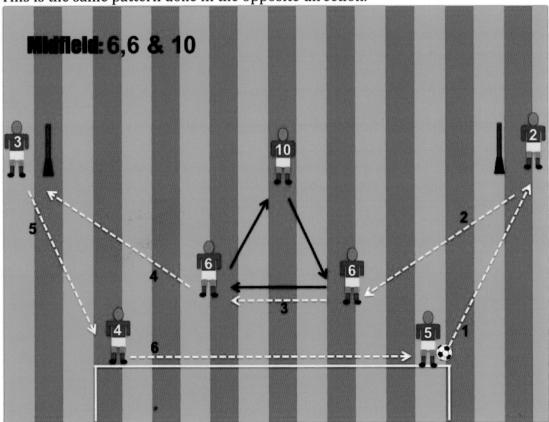

This next pattern uses combination play and rotation between three center-midfield players. The specific roles of each center midfielder is determined by the coach. The more rigid the tactics means the more restraints on the players, the more flexible and free the tactics, the less restraints on the players. Example: the coach may or may not assign a specific #6 & #8, instead letting the players fill the spaces where needed in the flow of the game. By giving players a basic framework (formation) and then allowing them the freedom to operate and make decisions inside that framework, makes the formation more flexible and less predictable.

The rotation in this pattern has the #10 switching with the #6. This is exactly the type of rotation that makes the formation less rigid and predictable, allowing a greater number of players more freedom to fill different spaces, instead of one player always filling up the same space. This pattern can be done using two variations: The #6 & #10 can inter-change after the 7th pass or they can inter-change after the 4th pass. Train the pattern in both directions.

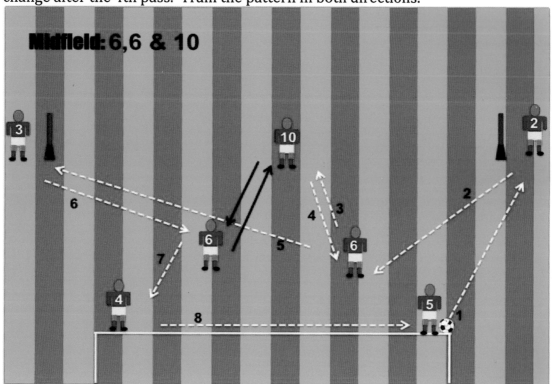

Midfield: 6,6 & 10

This pattern now has the #6 surge forward switching with the #10. Make sure the #6 and #10 time their movement together. Having the #6 come forward from deep will be hard for the defense to pick up. After each complete rotation the #10 and the #6 will start in opposite positions.

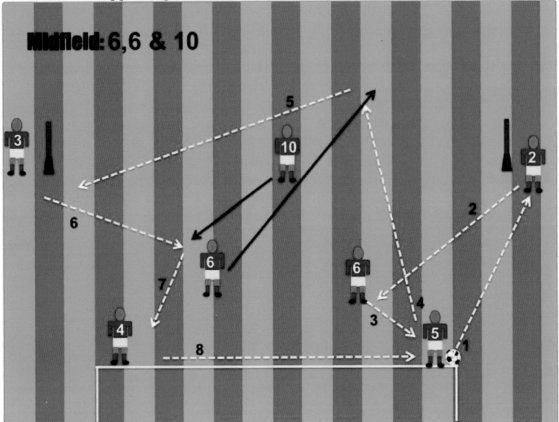

Center Midfield: 6-8-8 Variations

Now the team has two #8's and one #6. This pattern is a simple rotation off the ball, working it through the #6 & #8. In this example the #6 is the traditional swing player who rotates the ball but instead of one #8 there are two. This gives the #6 a triangle of passing options to work the ball out of the back.

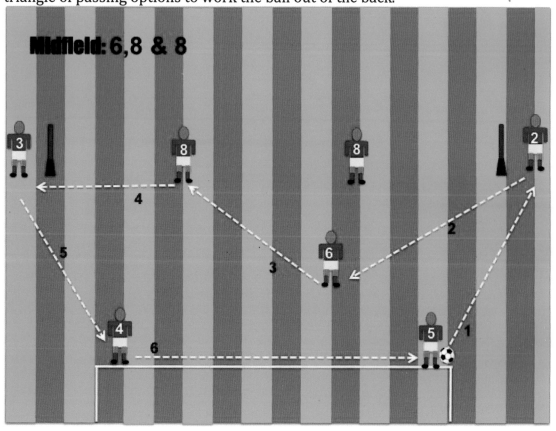

This is the same pattern done in the opposite direction.

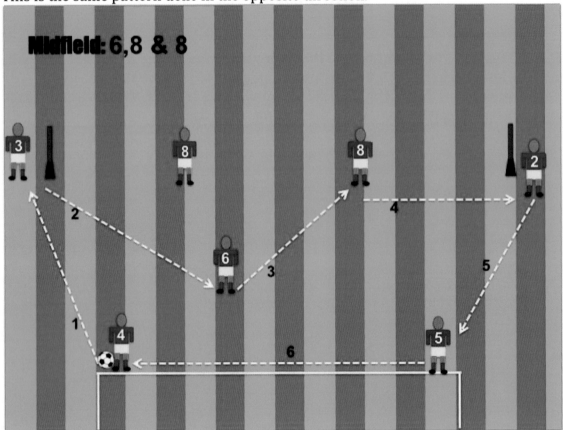

Here is an example of combination play between the #6 & #8's in the process of rotating the ball.

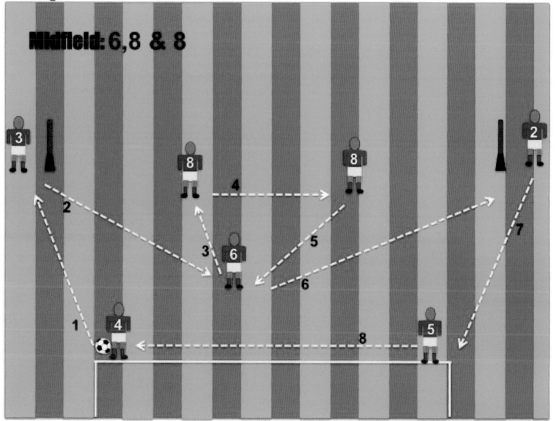

This example uses combination play and inter-changing of positions between the #6 & #8.

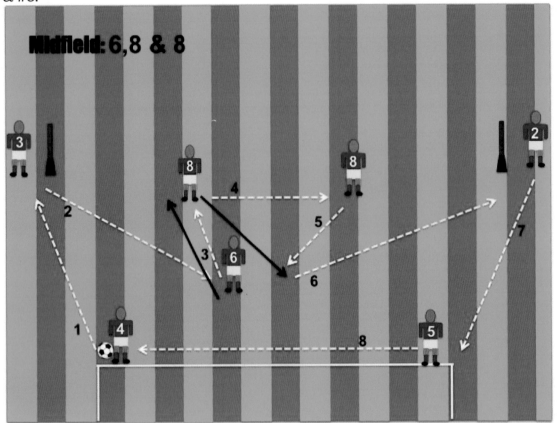

Center Midfield: 6-8-10 Variations

This set-up shows the center midfielders in a classic 4-2-3-1 formation with the 6,8 & 10 all spread-out in their familiar spaces. You can see the where the problems would arise if these players operated only in these specific spaces during the actual game. This pattern uses all three players in combination to rotate the ball.

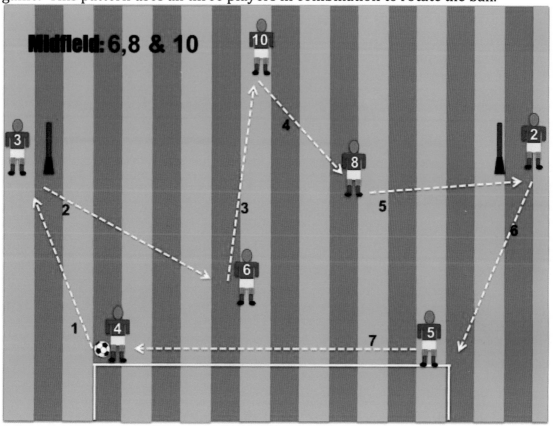

The #6,8 & 10 use a counterclockwise rotation as they all rotate one spot. They are still playing the classic #6,8 & 10 roles but the #10 becomes the #6, #6 becomes the #8 and the #8 becomes the #10. Each rotation will switch the player's position, allowing them to fill different spaces.

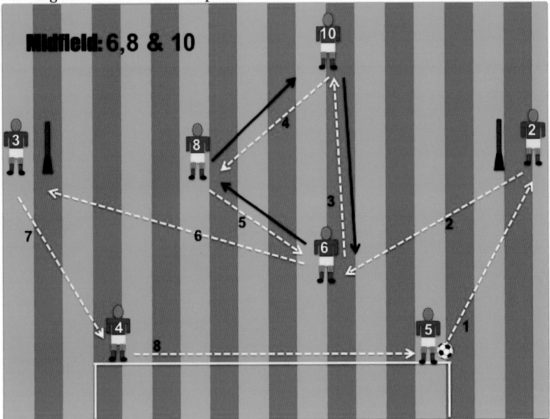

Center Midfield: 6-10-10 Variations

In this three-player combination pattern there is one #6 and two #10's. Having two #10's could be considered more attack minded because each of the #10's are in a position to surge forward quickly (it also gives the striker more support).

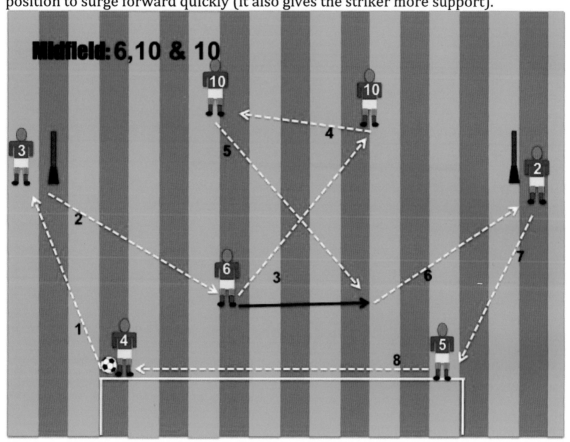

This pattern operates with two #10's as one of them drops slightly deeper to collect the pass from the #5 (CB). Eventually the two #10's will inter-change positions in during the pattern.

Midfield: 6,10 & 10

Back Four, #6 & #8

This pattern works the basic ball circulation of the back four and the #6 & #8. The idea of the pattern is to focus on firm accurate passing and receiving while circulating the ball at a high tempo. This pattern is not about teaching movement but rather a tempo passing exercise that trains technique.

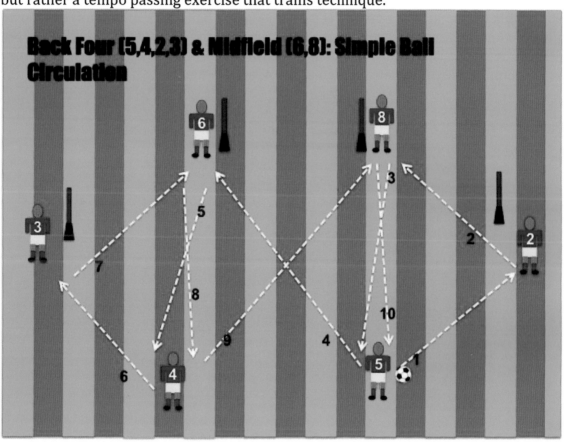

Center Backs, #6, #8 & Wingers

This pattern is designed to work on the movements of the #6, #8 and the wingers (#7 & #11). The winger's movement is diagonally inwards. This type of run by the wingers is designed to exploit the space between the opponents back line and midfield line while opening up the outside channels for the wingbacks to run into. The #6 & #8 take turns dropping deep to receive the ball as the other supports on a diagonal forward angle. Example: as the #6 receives the ball deeper, the #8 is closer to the blue stick on a forward diagonal angle (the reverse is true when the #8 drops deep). Emphasize timed coordinated movement between players.

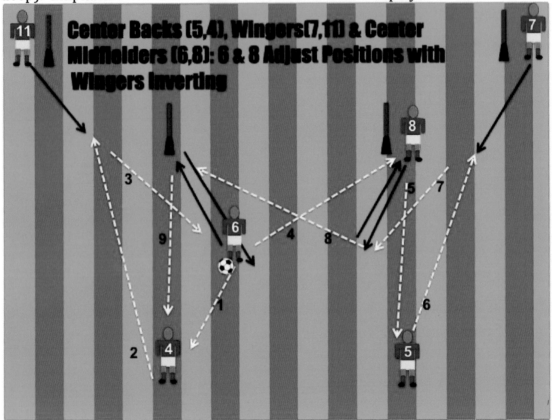

Wingers, Striker, #10, #8 & #3

This pattern begins to combine players from the backline all the way to the striker. The entire midfield except for the #6 is involved along with one wingback and the striker. The idea of the pattern is for the #9, #7, #11 and #10 to form a diamond shape as they sprint off their marks. When the #11 sprints inside it opens up room for the wingback (#3) to get down the channel to receive the ball from the #7. The wingback will play the ball back to the #8 and the pattern will start over. Notice there are two #3's, they will switch off every other repetition of the pattern. This will make it possible for the pattern to continuously run.

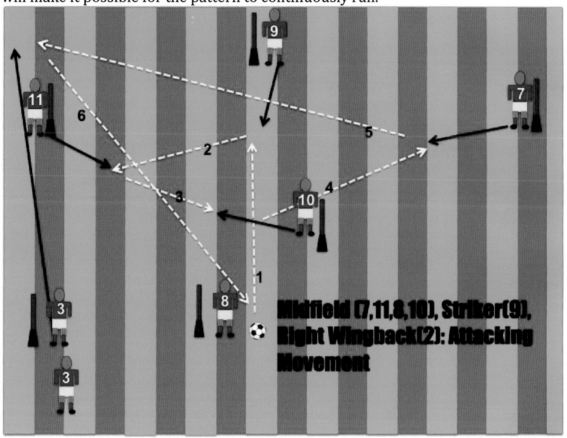

Midfield (7,11,8,10), Striker(9), Right Wingback(2): Attacking Movement

This pattern is the same as the previous but performed on the opposite side.

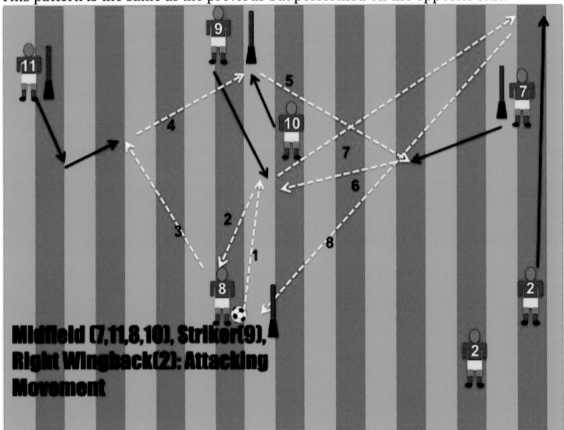

Midfield (7,11,8,10), Striker(9), Right Wingback(2): Attacking Movement

Back Four, #6, #8 & #10

Notice the how the 4-2-3-1 has now become a 2-1-3-1 in this attacking organization passing pattern. The #10 and #6 in this pattern serve to connect the lines.

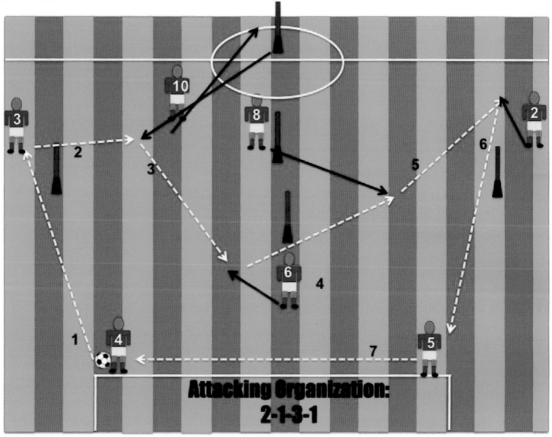

Attacking Organization: 2-1-3-1

Changing Team Shape In The 4-2-3-1 Formation

I use the term formation loosely because of the fluid way I view game. A team in a low defensive block (defensive organization phase) will take on a distinct compact shape, that shape will change when the ball is recovered and the team starts the attack (attacking transition). Attacking transition is simply those couple of seconds right when the ball is won. From attacking transition the opportunity to score quickly on the counter may or may not be available, if the opportunity to score quickly is not available, the team will again shift into a different shape called attacking organization. The attacking organization phase is when the team sets up to possess the ball and circulates the ball, trying to create an opportunity to score. When the ball is eventually lost in the attacking organization phase, the team will change shape again falling into what is called the defensive transition phase. The defensive transition phase is the moments right when the ball is lost. This entire process of constantly changing shape will be non-stop throughout the course of the game. Because this book is designed to stimulate movement ideas using passing patterns, pattern play and shadow play in the 4-2-3-1, I feel it is important to have an idea of what these changes in team shape will look like. By understanding how the 4-2-3-1 formation and all formations for that reason change shape, you will be better able to understand player movement. Ultimately, the idea I want to express is that formations are a basic framework or structure that serve to connect the players to a general idea of how the team plays (game model).

Attacking Organization: In this example, the 4-2-3-1 formation is transitioned into a 2-1-3-1-3 formation. This new attacking set-up makes circulating the ball much easier because the entire field is opened up. Notice how the wingbacks are pushed wide and high and the #6 & #10 are sitting in the gaps connecting the lines. From this starting position players can move to fill many different spaces, interchange positions, create attacking overloads and insure excellent movement off the ball while making it hard for the defense to make the field small.

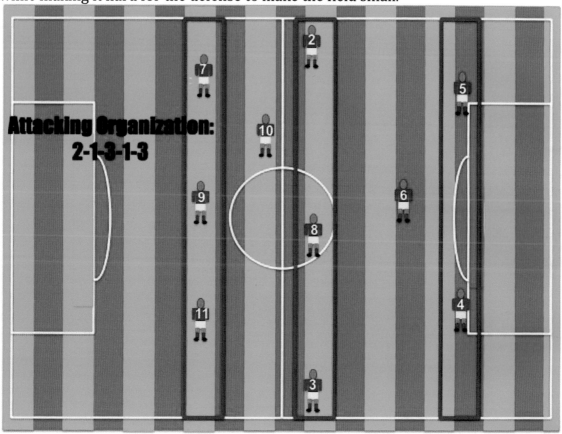

Attacking Organization/Transition: In this example, the 4-2-3-1 formation is transitioned into a 4-2-4. This shape is seen in attacking transition and can easily be adjusted to attacking organization, if the need to possess the ball and circulate it arises because there is not opportunity to score right away.

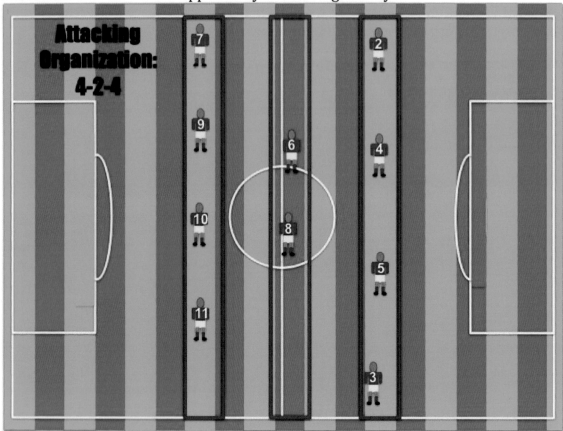

Defensive Organization: Notice how different this looks compared to the attacking examples. The shape of the team is completely different. The 4-1-4-1 set-up is very difficult to break down, especially with the #6 sitting in between the backline and midfield. Now imagine the transition required by the players as the phases of the game change (once they recover the ball).

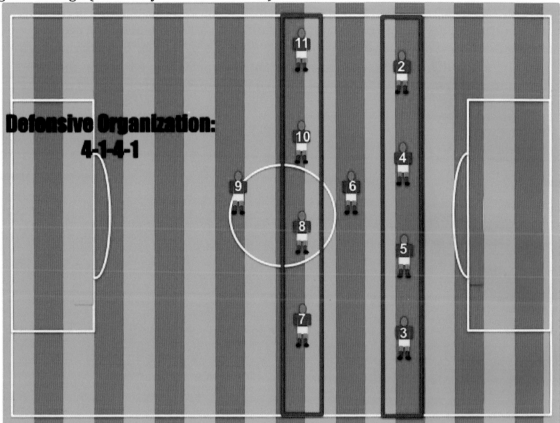

Defensive Organization:

This defensive shape now has two forwards that can pressure the opponents back four and no set player to cover between the back line and midfield line. There are many defensive tactics and set-ups you can teach, my intent here is simply to demonstrate how the 4-2-3-1 formation or any formation can change and needs to change. The coach can add structure to the formation by setting a line of confrontation, setting a line of restraint, deciding what are the pressing areas, handing out player specific responsibilities within the system and much more. Now when you are watching professional soccer and the formation comes on the television, don't be so quick to believe it! A simple 4-2-3-1 can be played in many different ways.

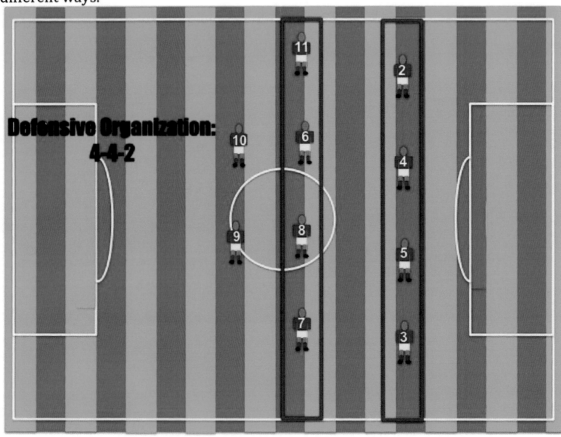

Team Passing Pattern: Full Field

Team passing patterns serve to tie all the movement ideas together in a full team setting. These patterns are game realistic working on total team movement, passing tempo and finishing. There are a number of different ways the team can train team-passing patterns.

In the below pattern the team will move up the field together, carrying out a pre-determined pattern that ends with a strike on goal. I find it effective to run through the pattern slowly a couple times and then have the players perform it at speed many times. After a sufficient amount of repetitions change the pattern. The coach should draw up many different team patterns in order to give the players an array of possible movements on the field. This specific pattern shows the team working the entire field but you can draw up patterns that can be worked in different spaces, it depends on what you are working on. Later in the book I give you examples of working in just the attacking 1/3.

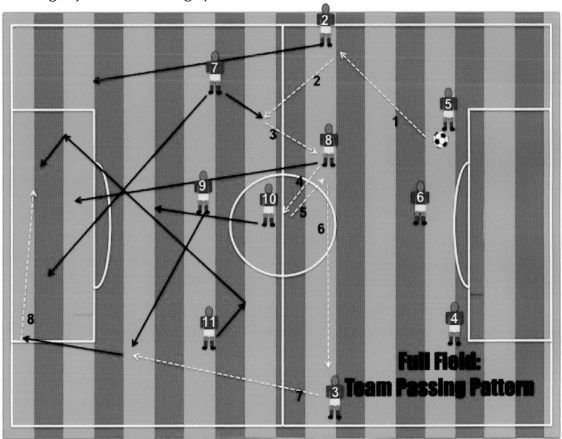

Full Field:
Team Passing Pattern

Team Passing Patterns: Half-Field Passing

This team pattern is set-up to rotate repetitions by side. The left wingback and winger are involved in the example below. After one repetition on the left the same pattern will be run on the right side with the right wingback and winger. The pattern you create will determine the exact players that will be involved. However, all players should be involved in at least one of the repetitions. Training patterns in this fashion is another way to teach team movement, which is different than the entire team working all at one time, like the previous example. I find both ways very useful and the players enjoy having pattern play mixed up. You may also find it useful to use cones that will serve to mark each players starting position. This gives a reference point for players as to where to begin.

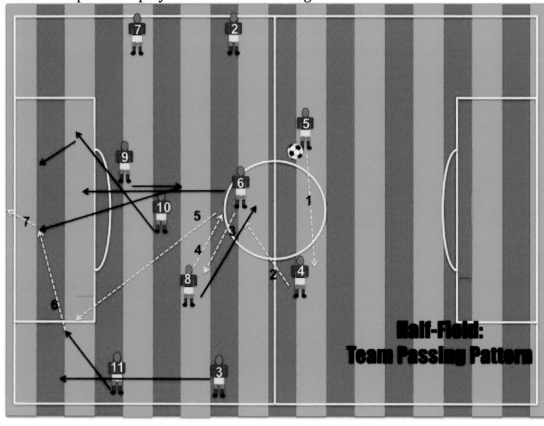

Using The Positional Grid To Train Shadow Play

The positional grid is something Pep Guardiola uses to teach team & player tactical positioning. I set this grid up on the field for my players to use during shadow play training. I like making grids on the field because it helps the players familiarize themselves with specific locations that they may not have done if the grid wasn't present. Example: when creating an attacking overload, it is very easy for players to see if two players are in a grid versus one player. When this occurs the players know they have created an attacking overload in that specific section. In a way it teaches players to look at the game in a different way. There are many uses for the positional grid, but in this book we are only looking at it for the purpose of teaching shadow play. Shadow play was introduced to me years ago in its most basic form, which was 11v0 working the ball freely and scoring on the opposite goal. However, as I studied shadow play I realized there are many effective ways it can be carried out. Shadow play is essentially about moving the ball in a way that trains your teams "game model" in a realistic fashion with the end result ending in an attempt on goal. Shadow play can be one team or two teams (working in opposite directions), against a limited number of opposition (semi-passive defenders) or working around mannequins. The coach can instruct the team to move the ball in specific directions, set specific pass requirements or let the team play with no restrictions. I recommend using a variety of shadow play methods.

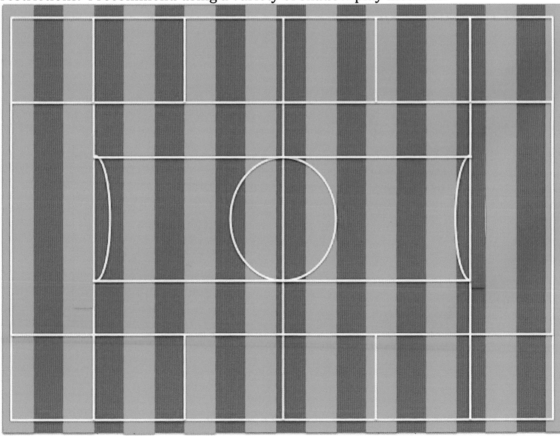

Position Grid: Color Coded

This positional grid is easily created on the field using different color cones placed in the center of each marked out grid. The outline of the entire grid is created using the lines already on the field along with one specific color cone.

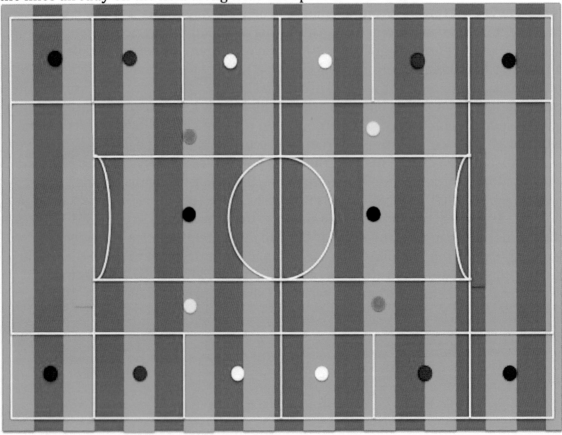

One Team Color Coded Shadow Play

This is an example of one team shadow play using the positional color-coded grid. The coach will call out the color grid the ball will be played into, the calling of colors will need to be logical and well paced in order to create a good passing tempo and realistic flow to the shadow play. After eight or more passes the coach can yell "finish". That will allow the team to freely attack the goal and score without the coaches calling of any more colors. Feel free to add variations as you see fit.

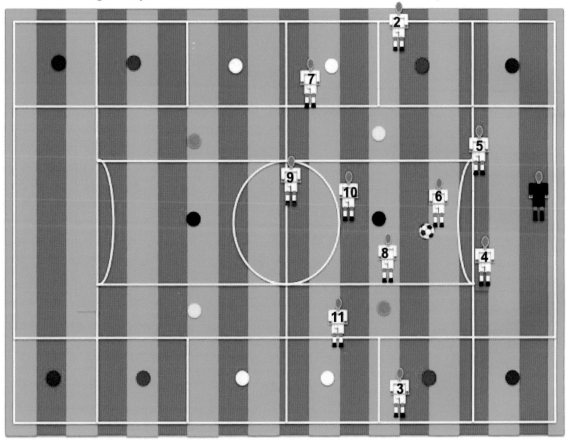

Two Team Color Coded Shadow Play

This is a variation of the previous one team color-coded shadow play. There are now two teams and two coaches on the field. Each team will have one coach who will call out specific color grids for their team to play into, each team will finish on the opposite goal when instructed (same as previous exercise). The nice thing about having two-team shadow play is it forces each team to be aware of the other team so they do not run into each other. It is a good way to ensure the players are always scanning the field with their heads up.

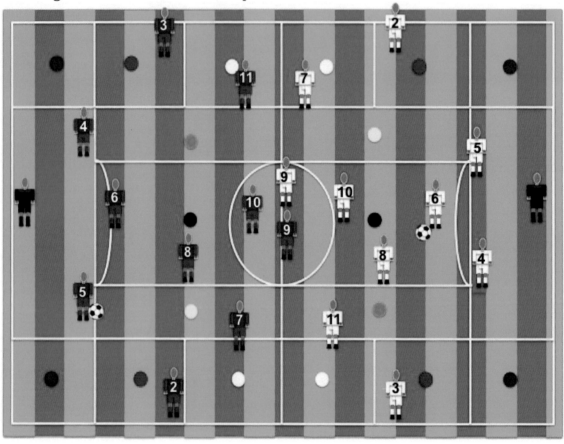

Color Coded 11v11 Game Play

Color-coded game play is a helpful practice method to use for both players and coaches. By identifying player partnerships in the 4-2-3-1 system using same color bibs, both players and coaches can now identify positioning & movement of partner players in the system. Notice how the red teams players are color coded by position (4+5,6+8,9+10, 2+7 & 3+11). By no means do I want to restrict movement by color-coding the player partnerships but it helps organize the movement in a visual sense easier.

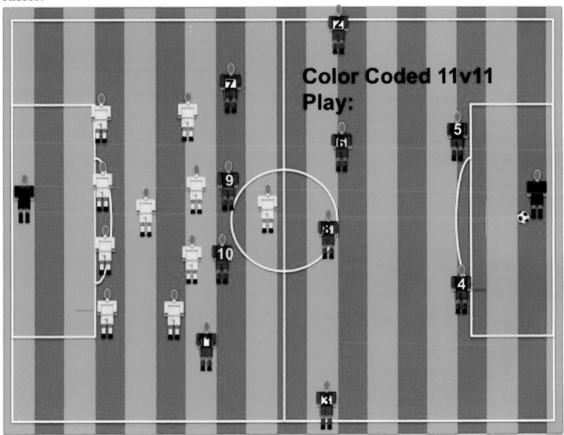

Color Coded 11v11 Play:

Color Coded Pattern Play

Color-coded pattern play is the same as pattern play but now the players are color-coded by their partnerships. In this example cones are used to mark starting positions for the players. You might find that using cones as starting points for players makes rehearsing patterns easier. The color-coding serves to make movement easier by visually coding the partnerships.

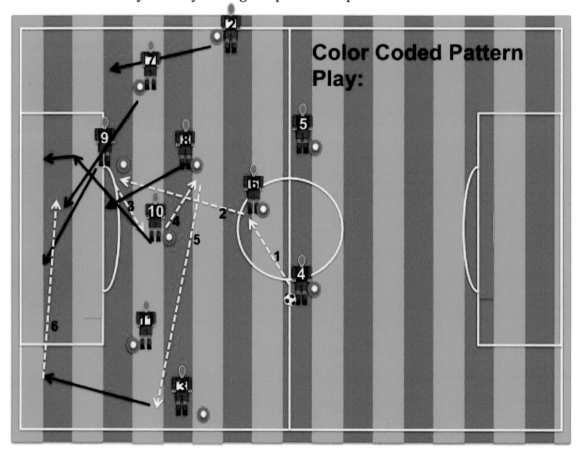

Attacking Patterns Using Split Field & Specific Players

This first attacking pattern focuses on the wingback, winger, attacking center mid, striker and passing center mid. The right side will attack first and then the left side, the pattern is run continuously with each side alternating reps. You can easily add another wingback, striker and attacking center mid – this will give the players more rest as they rotate every other repetition. In this specific example the wingback plays the ball into the #9 who is cutting towards the ball, the #9 lays the ball off to the #8, the #7 winger opens up wide to receive the ball from the #8, the #7 drives the end line and crosses the ball into the area looking for the #10 or #9 making their runs into the box. Having the #7 open up wide, the #10 & #9 interchange positions coordinating runs into the box with the #8 crashing the box. This type of pattern provides the players with good movement ideas.

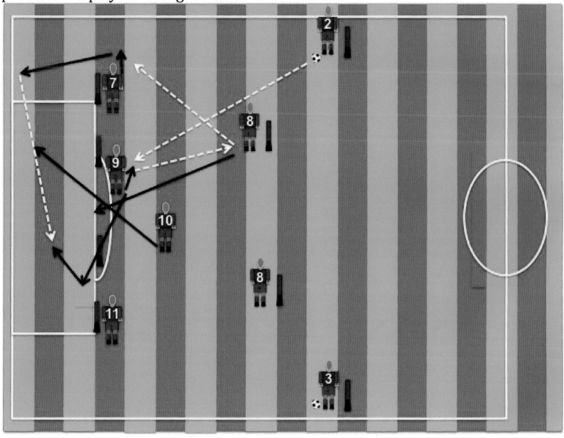

This pattern is a variation of the previous but the movement is adjusted. The wingback plays the ball into the #9 who lays the ball to the #8, at that point the pattern changes. The #8 plays the ball into the wingback that is sprinting down the sideline. The #7 instead of getting wide cuts across the back line (the blue sticks simulate the defensive back four) coordinating his run with the wingbacks run. The #10 & #9 coordinate their runs to cover near and far post as the #7 and #8 crash the box as well. The important part to this pattern is the coordinated timed movement of all players along with firm passing to the correct foot at all times. The next variation is to allow the #8 to choose the pass. If he wants to hit the #7 midfielder breaking across the defensive line he can or he can play the ball wide to the wingback running down the line.

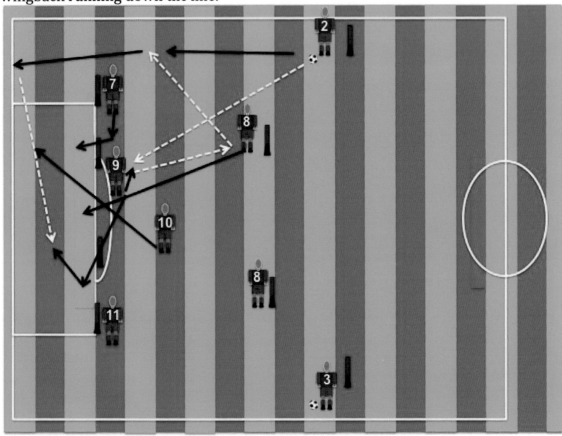

Here is the exercise with two wingbacks and two #9's & #10's. One pair (#9 + #10) will go with the right side repetition of the pattern and one pair will go with the left side. The wingbacks can take turns subbing in every other repetition. Now the pattern is color-coded as well.

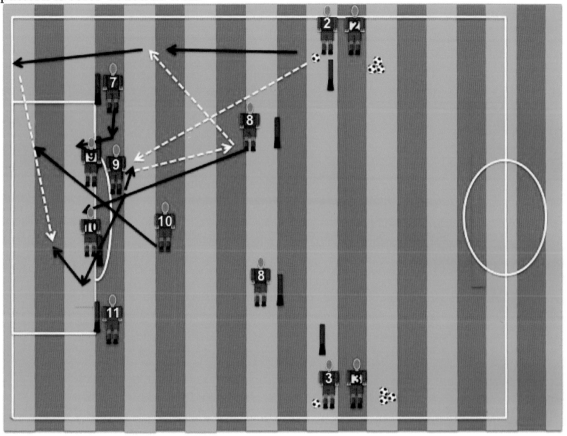

16121210R00025

Printed in Great Britain
by Amazon